15

15

The First
Moon Landing

Events That Shaped America

Sabrina Crewe and Dale Anderson

Gareth Stevens Publishing

A WORLD ALMANAC EDUCATION GROUP COMPANY

Please visit our web site at: www.garethstevens.com
For a free color catalog describing Gareth Stevens Publishing's list of high-quality
books and multimedia programs, call 1-800-542-2595 (USA) or 1-800-387-3178
(Canada). Gareth Stevens Publishing's fax: (414) 332-3567.

Library of Congress Cataloging-in-Publication Data available upon request from publisher.
Fax (414) 336-0157 for the attention of the Publishing Records Department.

ISBN 0-8368-3397-X

This North American edition first published in 2004 by
Gareth Stevens Publishing
A World Almanac Education Group Company
330 West Olive Street, Suite 100
Milwaukee, WI 53212 USA

This edition © 2004 by Gareth Stevens Publishing.

Produced by Discovery Books
Editor: Sabrina Crewe
Designer and page production: Sabine Beaupré
Photo researcher: Sabrina Crewe
Maps and diagrams: Stefan Chabluk
Gareth Stevens editorial direction: Jim Mezzanotte
Gareth Stevens art direction: Tammy Gruenewald

Photo credits: Corbis: pp. 4, 6, 9 (top), 11, 24; The New York Times Co./Library of
Congress: p. 19; NASA: cover, pp. 5, 7, 8, 9 (bottom), 10, 12, 13, 14, 15, 16, 17, 18,
20, 21, 22, 23, 25, 26; NASA/ACS Science Team: p. 27.

Printed in the United States of America

1 2 3 4 5 6 7 8 9 08 07 06 05 04

Contents

Introduction

One Giant Leap

At 10:56 P.M. Eastern Daylight Time on July 20, 1969, a large boot settled onto a powdery surface. As the foot came down, its owner said, "That's one small step for man, one giant leap for mankind."

The speaker was astronaut Neil Armstrong, and his step made him the first person to set foot on the Moon. Armstrong and two other astronauts were on a U.S. **lunar** space mission called *Apollo 11*—the first manned mission to land on the Moon. Back on Earth, millions of people were watching this amazing event on television.

Some footprints left on the Moon by astronauts are still there. The Moon has no wind to disturb them.

Exploring the Unknown

"This has been far more than three men on a voyage to the Moon. . . . This stands as a symbol of the insatiable curiosity of all mankind to explore the unknown."

Buzz Aldrin, Apollo 11 *astronaut, on his return to Earth, 1969*

President John F. Kennedy addresses Congress on May 25, 1961. He declared that the United States should land a person on the Moon before the end of the 1960s.

The Space Race

The journey lasted only a few days, but it was very important to the United States, which was competing with another powerful nation to see who would get to the Moon first. The **Soviet Union** had launched the first **satellite** into space and put the first human into **orbit** around Earth. Americans wanted to prove that they could achieve something even more dramatic in space, and they succeeded in doing so.

 An Impossible Dream

Before people had the **technology** to travel in space, they always wondered about the Moon. What was it made of? Was there life on the Moon? Most people knew nothing about Earth's place in the Solar System or the Moon's relationship to Earth. Even just fifty years ago, few would have believed it was possible to go to the Moon—that astronauts could get in a spacecraft, leave Earth's **atmosphere**, travel about 240,000 miles (385,000 kilometers), land on the Moon, and return safely. But humans have long been curious about what is beyond their world, and it is this curiosity that helped scientists achieve the seemingly impossible.

Chapter One

The Space Program

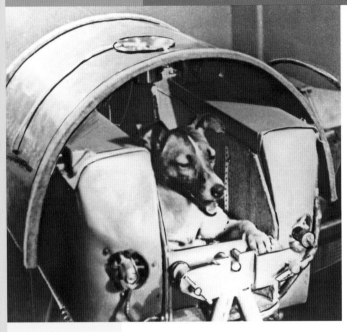

A dog named Laika was the first living creature sent into space from Earth. This photograph shows Laika inside *Sputnik II,* the craft that took her into space in 1957.

The First People in Space

On April 12, 1961, a person left Earth and went into space for the first time. Soviet **cosmonaut** Yuri Gagarin completed one orbit around Earth, sending back radio messages about what he felt and saw. Gagarin's 108-minute flight made him the world's first space hero. Valentina Tereshkova, who became the first woman in space in 1963, was also a Soviet.

Americans Follow

The first American in space was Alan Shepard. His flight on May 5, 1961, lasted only fifteen minutes and didn't take him into orbit. In early 1962—nearly a year after Gagarin's flight—John Glenn became the first American to orbit Earth. He was acclaimed as a hero, and about four million people showered him with tickertape during a parade in New York City.

Feeling Weightless

"I felt wonderful when the **gravity** pull began to disappear. . . . I suddenly found I could do things much more easily than before. And it seemed as though my hands and legs and my whole body did not belong to me. They did not weigh anything."

Yuri Gagarin describing space flight

The President Makes a Challenge

The U.S. space program is run by the National Aeronautics and Space Administration (NASA). In 1961, President Kennedy gave NASA a bold new mission. In a speech to Congress, the president said Americans should be the first to put a man on the Moon, and they should do it before the end of the 1960s.

A Bold Goal

"I believe that this nation should commit itself to achieving the goal, before this decade is out, of landing a man on the Moon and returning him safely to Earth. No single project in this period will be more impressive to mankind or more important for the long-range exploration of space."

President John F. Kennedy, speech to Congress, May 25, 1961

On May 5, 1961, the United States launched its first manned space flight, with Alan Shepard on board. The spacecraft reached an altitude of 116.5 miles (187.5 km).

Walking in Space
"This is the greatest experience; it's just tremendous. . . . Right now, I'm standing on my head and I'm looking right down and looks like we're coming up on the coast of California."

Edward White, describing his Gemini 4 *spacewalk, 1965*

How to Do It

It was NASA's job to design, build, and test spacecraft for a journey to the Moon. It also had to work out how the astronauts would perform certain important tasks. In 1965 and 1966, NASA tested different solutions to their problems with a series of missions called Project Gemini.

 Project Gemini

Astronauts on *Gemini 3* were the first to use an on-board computer to control the spacecraft. On *Gemini 4*, Edward White became the first American to walk in space. *Gemini 6* achieved the first **rendezvous**, or meeting, of two spacecraft. *Gemini 7* proved, with its fourteen-day voyage, that people could survive in space long enough to go to the Moon and back. *Gemini 8* managed **docking**, which is when spacecraft actually join in space.

The Apollo Program

After Gemini, the next step in the race to the Moon was the Apollo program. For Apollo, engineers designed a spacecraft with three modules, or pieces, that worked together. The **command module** (CM) made the long trips between Earth and the Moon. It held the instruments used to control the craft and the astronauts' living space. The **lunar module** (LM) made the shorter trip from the CM to the Moon's surface and back. The service module contained equipment, supplies, and the rocket that would send the CM back to Earth.

A Saturn V rocket launches *Apollo 11*. The command and service modules form just the tip of the huge spacecraft that left Earth. The lunar module is inside, just below the service module.

The Rocket

While the Apollo spacecraft was being designed, engineers made a rocket powerful enough to send the spacecraft to the Moon. The huge Saturn V rocket was 36 stories high and weighed 5.8 million pounds (2.6 million kilograms).

The hub of Mission Control was one large room, constantly manned by one of four teams of flight controllers.

Controlling the Flight

Spacecraft in the Apollo program were launched from the Kennedy Space Center in Florida. After the launch, Mission Control in Houston, Texas, took control of the missions. Mission Control was a busy station where scientists and

Technology in the 1960s

In the 1960s, many things that we now take for granted in the home, office, and factory were still being developed. People still had black-and-white televisions. Nobody had computers at home—these machines took up whole rooms, but they couldn't do what the simplest personal computer can do today. In 1958, however, the silicon chip had been invented. Although tiny, it could process information and control all kinds of devices, especially computers, and a computer was installed on *Apollo 11*. After the silicon chip, technology advanced so fast over the next few years that an astronaut on the last Apollo mission carried a pocket calculator more powerful than the *Apollo 11* computer.

engineers kept track of all the different systems on board the spacecraft, such as the engines, guidance, and life support. Doctors monitored the astronauts' health by reading results sent back from the spacecraft. Top managers advised the astronauts on how to **navigate**, conduct experiments, and solve any problems that arose.

On Earth, the capsule communicator, or "capcom," was the link between Mission Control and the astronauts in flight. The capcom was always another astronaut, someone who understood what it felt like to be an astronaut in space.

Many Missions

NASA flew ten Apollo missions before it felt ready to land people on the Moon. There had been some accidents, and it was important to make sure all the equipment worked as planned. Before risking a landing on the Moon, everything had to be tested one more time, by traveling around the Moon itself. In May 1969, *Apollo 10* carried out those tests successfully.

This view of the *Apollo 10* command module above the Moon's surface was taken from the lunar module after the two spacecraft did a test separation.

Chapter Two

Apollo 11

A Rough Ride

"It was, I thought, quite a rough ride in the first fifteen seconds or so. . . . I don't mean that the engines were rough, and I don't mean that it was noisy. But it was very busy—that's the best word. It was steering like crazy. . . . But the jerkiness quieted down after about fifteen seconds."

Michael Collins, describing the liftoff of Apollo 11

Ready at Last

NASA was satisfied with the test results of *Apollo 10*, and it decided that the next mission, *Apollo 11*, would try to land on the Moon. Neil Armstrong commanded *Apollo 11* and was also the pilot of the lunar module, the *Eagle*. Buzz Aldrin, a scientist, was in the LM with Armstrong. Michael Collins piloted the command module, *Columbia*.

Liftoff!

On the morning of July 16, 1969, about eight thousand special guests and two thousand journalists filled the viewing stands near the

The astronauts that went on the first mission to land on the Moon were (left to right) Neil Armstrong, Michael Collins, and Buzz Aldrin.

Everyday Life in Space

Inside the command module, as elsewhere in space, the astronauts were weightless because there was no gravity. They floated around the cabin and had to strap or wedge themselves in place when they slept or if they just wanted to stay put.

The astronauts lived on freeze-dried meals—such as chicken stew —and sandwiches. They snacked on dried fruit and drank cold drinks and coffee.

Since there was no bathroom in the capsule, the astronauts used special plastic bags for their urine and bowel movements. Although they could shave, they could not wash with soap and water and had to use wipes and tissues instead.

This picture was taken minutes after the launch of *Apollo 11*. It shows the Saturn V's first stage, which has used up its fuel, dropping away from the spacecraft.

Kennedy Space Center. Nearly one million people lined the Florida beaches, and hundreds of millions around the world watched on television as the Saturn V rocket began to roar, carrying *Apollo 11* into the sky.

Just twelve minutes after the launch, *Apollo 11* was speeding along at 17,400 miles (28,000 km) per hour and had begun to orbit Earth. In under three hours, *Apollo 11* had left Earth's orbit and turned toward the Moon. *Apollo 11* was on its way.

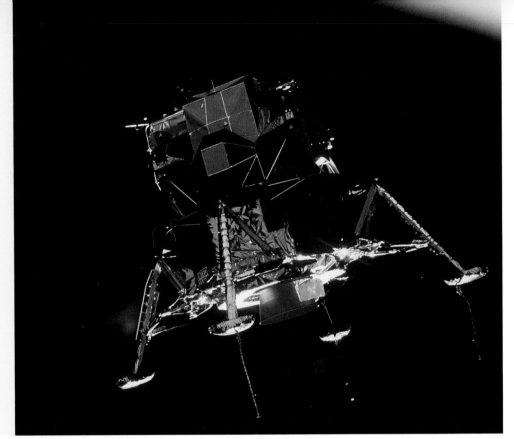

A photograph taken from the command module records the exciting moment when the *Eagle*, shown here, went into orbit around the Moon. You can see a small part of the Moon in the top right corner of the picture.

Getting Close

After three days in space, *Apollo 11* started to orbit the Moon. It was time for the *Eagle*—the LM that would land on the Moon with Armstrong and Aldrin—to separate from the CM. Collins, in the CM *Columbia*, would stay in orbit and wait for the other two astronauts to come back up.

The separation of the two modules was successful, and Armstrong and Aldrin were now on their own. Armstrong told Mission Control, "The *Eagle* has wings." He meant that the LM was on its way to the Moon.

Descent

On July 20, 1969, the *Eagle* began a descent toward its destination, an area of the Moon called the Sea of Tranquility. Computers controlled the descent. But at about 30,000 feet (9,000 meters) above the surface, alarms began to sound, telling the crew that the computers had too much information to process. Aldrin and Armstrong spent a few moments getting the situation under control. When Armstrong looked outside again, he saw they were about 1,000 feet (300 m) from the ground and heading for a crater filled with rocks!

Landing on the Moon

Armstrong moved the LM away from danger and began looking for a safe place to land. At last, with only seven seconds of fuel left, the LM made a good landing. A few moments later, Neil Armstrong said his first famous words on the Moon, "Houston, Tranquility Base here. The *Eagle* has landed." Charley Duke, the capcom that day, revealed the tension felt at Mission Control with his reply: "You've got a bunch of guys [down here] about to turn blue. We're breathing again."

One Small Step

Armstrong and Aldrin were supposed to get some sleep before they left the LM, but they were too excited. A few hours after landing, and having made many checks and preparations, the astronauts left the LM. A camera on the outside of the craft sent pictures—seen by millions on Earth—of Armstrong climbing down the ladder and stepping onto the lunar surface, the first person on the Moon. Aldrin, who followed, described the Moon landscape as "magnificent desolation."

On the Moon, Neil Armstrong holds the flagpole of a U.S. flag as Buzz Aldrin adjusts the mounting. The flag had a rod running through the top to hold it up because there is no wind on the Moon.

Moonwalking

Armstrong and Aldrin's moonwalk lasted about two hours. Getting around on the Moon was no easy matter because it has much less gravity than Earth. The astronauts had to lean forward in the direction they wanted to go and then take a few steps to build up speed. To stop, they had to slow down ahead of time or else overshoot their destination.

In spite of the difficulties, Armstrong and Aldrin got a great deal of work done. They collected rocks to be analyzed on Earth and set up various scientific experiments.

After the astronauts took a walk around the Moon, they left some mementos. They set up an American flag and a plaque that reads, "Here men from the planet Earth first set foot upon the Moon, July 1969 A.D. We came in peace for all mankind." They also left tributes honoring Soviet and American astronauts who had died while they were working in the space program.

The steel plaque commemorating the *Apollo 11* landing was bolted onto the landing gear of the lunar module. The bottom part of the LM, with its plaque, remains on the Moon today.

The Big Test

On July 21, the astronauts got ready to leave. Back at Mission Control, people were very nervous because it was the first time anyone had tried a space launch from a place other than Earth. If anything went wrong, two lives were at risk. Aboard the CM, Collins worried that he would not be able to rescue the others if there was an accident.

Everyone was relieved when the rockets fired up, just as they should. The top part of the LM separated from the bottom part, as planned, to take Armstrong and Aldrin back into orbit around the Moon. Once in orbit, the *Eagle* caught up with *Columbia*.

Coming Home

The two craft docked successfully, and the LM astronauts re-boarded *Columbia*. Once safely back in the CM, the crew discarded the *Eagle* because it was no longer needed. They fired the engine that would take them out of lunar orbit and home to Earth. *Apollo 11* finished its eight-day journey when the CM splashed down in the Pacific Ocean on July 24, 1969.

On July 24, after splash-down, the astronauts got out of the battered CM and into a life raft. Then they waited for a helicopter to collect them.

Playing Safe

As soon as they emerged from *Columbia*, Armstrong, Aldrin, and Collins were placed in **quarantine**. Scientists did not know if there were any microscopic forms of life on the Moon that could be dangerous to plants, animals, or humans on Earth. Just in case, the three astronauts were kept in a trailer at Mission Control, apart from everyone else, for two weeks.

A Big Welcome

The astronauts of *Apollo 11* were hailed as great heroes around the world. When they got out of quarantine, Armstrong, Aldrin, and Collins were honored in a tickertape parade in New York City and at a state dinner with U.S. president Richard Nixon. These events were just two of many across the United States that celebrated their astonishing achievement. Next, the astronauts went on a whirlwind tour around the world, this time on land.

The *Apollo 11* astronauts share a joke with President Nixon from inside their quarantine trailer.

The day after the Moon landing, *The New York Times* gave its whole front page to the historic event.

Skeptics and Believers

Some people did not believe that people had reached the Moon. They thought it was a trick of television because it simply wasn't possible to go to the Moon and back. Other people in some areas of the world said it was a piece of false information put out by the U.S. government to make the nation look more powerful than the Soviet Union. They were convinced the whole thing had been staged in a remote desert somewhere in the United States.

On the other hand, many people were excited and thought they, too, might go to the Moon. About ninety thousand people wrote to the airline Pan American World Airways for reservations on the first commercial flight to the Moon, then planned for the year 2000.

Chapter Three

Moon Science

Apollo Continues

NASA sent six more Apollo missions to the Moon after *Apollo 11*. The first of these six, *Apollo 12*, left Earth on November 14, 1969. On these missions, the astronauts performed experiments, tested new equipment, and gathered much useful information.

Old Rocks and New Minerals

Apollo astronauts who went to the Moon brought back rocks for scientists on Earth to examine. Some were older than any found on Earth. Others contained minerals never before seen. One of these minerals was named "armalcolite" after the three astronauts of *Apollo 11* ("arm" for Armstrong, "al" for Aldrin,

David Scott, *Apollo 15* commander, has set up all kinds of experiments on the Moon. Around him are bores and drills for exploring beneath the Moon's surface.

Later Apollo missions used lunar rovers to get around on the Moon. This rover chugged along at 9 miles (14 km) per hour.

"col" for Collins, and "ite" because it is a mineral). This mineral came from **meteorites** that had hit the Moon's surface. Later, it was found in craters left by meteorites that had hit Earth.

The Moon's early history reveals information about the formation of Earth, Mars, Venus, and Mercury. The astronauts' rock samples and other tests showed the Moon and the Earth had similar origins and were made of similar materials.

Water and Life on the Moon?

Because the Moon has no atmosphere, there is no air and no temperature control—it is baking hot in the heat of the Sun and gets freezing cold at night. There are no living creatures, nor any evidence that anything has ever lived there. In 1998, however, the possibility of water—and therefore the potential for life—was detected on the Moon.

The Drive to Explore

"Nothing will stop us. The road to the stars is steep and dangerous. But we're not afraid. . . . Space flights can't be stopped. This isn't the work of any one man or even a group of men. It is a historical process which mankind is carrying out in accordance with the natural laws of human development."

Soviet cosmonaut Yuri Gagarin, 1967

Chapter Four

After Apollo

U.S. astronaut Donald Slayton and Soviet cosmonaut Aleksey Leonov during the Apollo-Soyuz mission.

Cooperation in Space

In the early 1970s, President Nixon began a new policy of peaceful cooperation with the Soviet Union. This policy led to the first international space mission.

The two nations needed three years to prepare for the mission. After much work, on July 17, 1975, history was made. A U.S. Apollo spacecraft docked in space with the Soviet *Soyuz 19*, and their crews met and exchanged a historic handshake. Once in orbit together, the two crews practiced different docking maneuvers, carried out experiments, ate together, and exchanged gifts.

The Hope of Apollo-Soyuz

"How this new era will go depends on the determination, commitment and faith of the people of both our countries and the world."

Tom Stafford, U.S. commander of Apollo-Soyuz

The First U.S. Space Station

NASA, meanwhile, was working on a space station called *Skylab*. Launched in May 1973, it could carry enough oxygen, water, and food for crews to stay for long periods of time.

Skylab was a very successful scientific station. Crews carried out medical studies of humans and biological studies of mice, fish, and spiders. They studied Earth's resources, such as fishing grounds and underground water, and took photographs of the Sun. They also manufactured new metals and used eight telescopes to capture images not available from Earth. The last crew left in February 1974. *Skylab* eventually lost its orbit, and in July 1979 the station fell back to Earth.

 ## Life on Skylab

Three crews traveled to *Skylab*, where life was much more comfortable than on the Apollo spacecraft. The station was about as large as a three-bedroom house. Food was frozen or canned instead of dried, and the astronauts had ovens and hot plates for cooking. Astronauts could wear ordinary clothes inside the station—pressure suits were now only needed for spacewalks and travel to and from Earth. They had sleeping bags hung on the walls and a special shower, toilet, and sink. Crew members could use a stationary bike to exercise so their muscles would not get weak from lack of use. During the last mission, astronauts stayed on *Skylab* for eighty-four days.

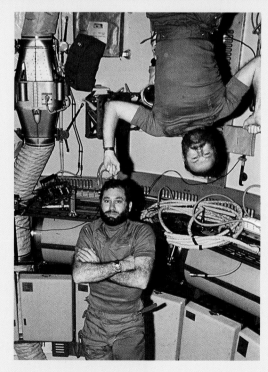

Two *Skylab* crew members demonstrate the fun of being weightless.

The Space Shuttle

Starting in 1981, NASA's main vehicle for space travel became the Space Shuttle. Shuttles are attached to launcher rockets for liftoff and are flown back to Earth like gliders, making their landings on a runway. The Shuttles can carry huge things into space, such as satellites or entire laboratories. Each Shuttle has a giant robotic arm with a "hand" at the end that astronauts can use to grab and move large objects.

Shuttle crews conduct experiments in biology, astronomy, engineering, and medicine. They have sent **probes** toward other planets and captured, repaired, and relaunched satellites. Missions are carried out for the government, for scientists and businesses, and for other countries around the world.

Challenger and *Columbia*

There have been two disasters that took the lives of Shuttle crews. On January 28, 1986, *Challenger* exploded in the sky, minutes after liftoff. On February 1, 2003, *Columbia* was returning from a mission when it broke into pieces.

Space Shuttles are launched with two rockets (one is visible on the right) and a huge tank of fuel (the red tank in the middle), all of which drop back to Earth once the Shuttle is in space.

In this picture of the International Space Station, you can see the huge robotic arm (right) that was Canada's contribution to the project. When it is finished, the ISS will be the size of two or three small houses.

The International Space Station

The International Space Station (ISS), launched in 1998, is a joint project of the United States, Russia, Canada, Japan, and the European Space Agency (which includes most countries of western Europe). The ISS is made up of different modules, such as a laboratory and a living space, joined together. Solar panels convert the Sun's energy into power to run the space station.

Living in Space

Astronauts from different countries have been living at the ISS since November 2000. Crews stay at the station for about five months before a new crew arrives to replace them. They conduct experiments in biology, space medicine, physics, and other fields. A "lifeboat"— an extra spacecraft—is docked at the station at all times in case the crew has to leave in an emergency.

A Worldwide Effort

"The station is the largest international engineering project ever undertaken in space, and it is the first truly global space exploration effort. Its unprecedented scale . . . will be matched . . . by the scale of the benefits its research will bring to lives on Earth."

Tommy Holloway, International Space Station Program Manager

Conclusion

A New View of Earth

"To see the Earth as it truly is, small and blue and beautiful in that eternal silence where it floats, is to see ourselves as riders on the Earth together, brothers on that bright loveliness in the eternal cold— brothers who know now that they are truly brothers."

Archibald MacLeish, Pulitzer-prizewinning writer and Librarian of Congress, after seeing the first pictures of Earth from space, 1968

Learning from Space

The space program has produced many benefits. Today, satellites are used to track the weather, see how crops are growing, and make more accurate maps. They give directions to ships' pilots, help control pollution, and protect nations. Scientific knowledge has advanced, thanks to the opportunity to study Moon rocks and the many experiments carried out by astronauts.

Advances in Technology

In everyday life, we use many things originally invented for use in space. People with diabetes, for example, now get the insulin they need through a small pump they wear on their belt. This idea came from the space program. The water filters developed for spacecraft have been adapted to purify drinking water in the home. We have powerful, fast computers today because the space program encouraged their development. Even sneakers are better today because shoe designers adapted ideas first used for astronauts.

Opening Up the Universe

Before the space program began, we already knew that Earth is part of a Solar System, revolving around a huge, glowing ball of gas we call the Sun. We also knew that our Sun is one of millions and millions of similar suns, or stars, in a galaxy that we call the Milky Way. And we knew there were many other galaxies beyond our own.

So what has the space program, including the Apollo missions to the Moon, taught us about the Universe? It has given scientists new information about the age and formation of our world, Solar System, and galaxy. It has also developed the Hubble Space Telescope, which orbits Earth and gets a much better view of space than any other telescope. In recent years, Hubble has shown us there are not millions, but *billions* of galaxies beyond our own. Above all, it has revealed something even more exciting—that there is a lot more to learn and discover.

The Hubble Space Telescope has enabled us to see farther into the Universe than ever before. These two galaxies, seen in an image sent back to Earth from the Hubble, are named "the Mice" because of their long tails of gas and stars.

Time Line

1961	April 12: Soviet cosmonaut Yuri Gagarin becomes first person in space.
	May 5: Alan Shepard becomes first American in space.
	May 25: President John F. Kennedy sets goal of putting a person on the Moon.
1962	February 20: John Glenn becomes first American to orbit Earth.
1963	June 16: Soviet cosmonaut Valentina Tereshkova becomes first woman in space.
1965	June 3: Edward White becomes first American to walk in space.
1969	May: *Apollo 10* carries out final tests for a Moon landing.
	July 16: *Apollo 11* lifts off from Florida and heads to the Moon.
	July 19: *Apollo 11* reaches lunar orbit.
	July 20: Armstrong and Aldrin land and walk on the Moon.
	July 21: *Eagle* leaves Moon, docks with *Columbia*.
	July 24: *Apollo 11* splashes down in the Pacific Ocean.
	November 14: *Apollo 12* mission is launched.
1973	May 14: U.S. launches *Skylab* space station into orbit.
1974	November 16–February 8: *Skylab 4*, longest American space mission to date.
1975	July 17: *Apollo 18* and *Soyuz 19* meet in first international space docking.
1979	July 11: *Skylab* space station falls to Earth.
1981	April 12–14: First launch, orbit, and landing of a Space Shuttle.
1986	January 28: Space Shuttle *Challenger* explodes after liftoff.
1990	Hubble Space Telescope is launched.
1998	December 6: First two pieces of International Space Station are joined together.
2003	February 1: Space Shuttle *Columbia* breaks apart on reentry.

Things to Think About and Do

On the Moon

Imagine it is 1969 and you are on the first flight to the Moon. You are in charge of communicating with Mission Control back on Earth. Describe what it feels like to be in the lunar module as it makes the final descent to the Moon. Then take a walk around on the Moon's surface and describe what you do and see. What does it feel like? How does Earth look from there?

Living in Space

Find out as much as you can about life in the International Space Station—NASA's web site has a lot of good information. Write a journal as if you were spending a day visiting the International Space Station. What did you wear and eat? Who did you meet? How did it feel being weightless?

How Big Is Big?

When you think about space, it's hard to understand the vast scale of the Universe because it is all so much bigger than we can picture in our minds. Divide a piece of paper into four squares by drawing lines. In one square, draw a circle that represents Earth. In the next square, draw another circle for the Solar System and mark the Sun, Earth, and the other planets inside it. In the third square, draw an oval to represent the Milky Way (our galaxy), and fill it with tiny dots to show as many solar systems as you can. Finally, in your last square, draw any shape you like and fill it with more tiny dots to represent all the billions of galaxies in the Universe. What does this help you realize about the size of our world?

Glossary

atmosphere:	layer of gases and water vapor around Earth that provides living things with oxygen, traps warmth and moisture, and protects Earth from damaging rays of the Sun.
command module:	also called CM. Section of the lunar spacecraft that carried astronauts from Earth to the Moon and back. In *Apollo 11*, it was named *Columbia*.
cosmonaut:	term used in the Soviet Union, and now Russia, for an astronaut.
dock:	join two spacecraft together.
gravity:	pull of Earth or other body that keeps things on the ground.
lunar:	having to do with the Moon.
lunar module:	also called LM. Section of the lunar spacecraft that astronauts used to travel between the CM and the Moon's surface. In *Apollo 11*, it was named the *Eagle*.
meteorite:	rock from space that lands on Earth, other planets, or moons.
navigate:	use scientific instruments and star positions to plot a course for a ship, plane, or spacecraft.
orbit:	travel in a circle around another object.
probe:	unmanned spacecraft, sent from Earth to another place in the Solar System, that sends back information to Earth.
quarantine:	separation of one or more persons from others in case they are carrying germs that cause disease.
rendezvous:	moving and steering of two spacecraft near each other for docking.
satellite:	object that orbits some other object in the Universe. The Moon is a satellite of Earth, and many manmade satellites also orbit Earth.
Soviet Union:	formerly unified group of states in eastern Europe and Asia—including Russia—that has now separated into individual nations.
technology:	knowledge, ability, and tools that improve ways of doing practical things.

Further Information

Books

Dyson, Marianne. *Home on the Moon: Living on a Space Frontier*. National Geographic, 2003.

Kelly, Nigel. *The Moon Landing: The Race Into Space* (Point of Impact). Heinemann Library, 2001.

Lassieur, Allison. *Astronauts* (True Books). Children's Press, 2000.

Mitton, Jacqueline, and Simon Mitton. *The Scholastic Encyclopedia of Space*. Scholastic, 1999.

Spangenburg, Ray, Kit Moser, and Diane Moser. *The Hubble Space Telescope* (Out of This World). Franklin Watts, 2002.

Web Sites

history.nasa.gov/ap11ann/ NASA's *Apollo 11* thirtieth anniversary web site offers picture galleries, original documents, audio tapes, video clips, and more about *Apollo 11*.

spaceflight.nasa.gov NASA information about living in space, the International Space Station, and the Space Shuttle, as well as current news pages.

www.solarviews.com/eng/history.htm The history of space exploration is offered in reports of missions from the beginning of the space program to those planned for the future.

Useful Addresses

National Aeronautics and Space Administration (NASA)
300 E Street, SW
Washington, DC 20546
Telephone: (202) 358-0000

National Air and Space Museum Information Center
7th and Independence Avenue, SW
Washington, DC 20560
Telephone: (202) 357-2700

Index

Page numbers in **bold** indicate pictures.